First World War
and Army of Occupation
War Diary
France, Belgium and Germany

39 DIVISION
Divisional Troops
E Squadron South Irish Horse
16 March 1916 - 30 April 1916

WO95/2574/1

The Naval & Military Press Ltd
www.nmarchive.com
Published in association with The National Archives

Published by

The Naval & Military Press Ltd

Unit 10 Ridgewood Industrial Park,

Uckfield, East Sussex,

TN22 5QE England

Tel: +44 (0) 1825 749494

www.naval-military-press.com

www.nmarchive.com

This diary has been reprinted in facsimile from the original. Any imperfections are inevitably reproduced and the quality may fall short of modern type and cartographic standards.

© **Crown Copyright**
Images reproduced by permission of The National Archives, London, England, 2015.

Contents

Document type	Place/Title	Date From	Date To
Heading	WO95/2574 Mar 16-Apr 16 E Sqd. S. Irish Horse		
Heading	Qdn Sth Irish Horse Mar-Apr 1916		
Heading	E Squad Vol I		
War Diary	Havre Brouck	16/03/1916	23/03/1916
War Diary	La Heye (St Vessart)	24/03/1916	31/03/1916
War Diary	La Haye	01/04/1916	16/04/1916
War Diary	Le Vertannoy	17/04/1916	30/04/1916

WO95/2574

(1)

Mar '16 — Ap. '16
E Sqd. S. Irish Horse

9TH DIVISION

QDN STH IRISH HORSE.

MAR - APR 1916.

I CORPS

E Sewall
s/ Lease
Vol I

Army Form C. 2118.

WAR DIARY
or
INTELLIGENCE SUMMARY
(Erase heading not required.)

E Sqdn 5th South Hants 39th Divisional Cavalry. In the field

Place	Date	Hour	Summary of Events and Information	Remarks and references to Appendices
Hazebrouck	16.3.16	—	Arrived Hazebrouck & got fixed up in Billets	
"	17.3.16	—	Divisional training. Was visited by the G.O.C. 39th Division	
"	18.3.16	—	" "	
"	19.3.16	—	" "	
"	20.3.16	—	" "	
"	21.3.16	—	" "	
"	22.3.16	—	" "	
"	23.3.16	—	" "	
La Hove (St Venant)	24.3.16	—	Left Hazebrouck 1pm 24th March 16 & marched to La Haye (St Venant) via Morbecque	
"	25.3.16	—	Standecamp. Divisional training	
"	26.3.16	—	" "	
"	27.3.16	—	" " visited by the G.O.C. 39th Division	
"	28.3.16	—	" "	
"	29.3.16	—	" "	
"	30.3.16	—	" "	
"	31.3.16	—	" "	

MJ Jacobs Capt
O.C. 39th Divisional Cavalry

Army Form C. 2118.

WAR DIARY
or
INTELLIGENCE SUMMARY
(Erase heading not required.)

XXIX

E.S.I House Vol 2

Place	Date	Hour	Summary of Events and Information	Remarks and references to Appendices
LA HAYE	1/2/17	—	Divisional training	
"	2nd	"	"	
"	3rd	"	"	
"	4th	"	"	1 Sergt attached to Divisional H'Qrs for temporary duty. 1 N.C.O. & 7 men attached to H'Qrs 1st Army for Rail Duty
"	5th	"	"	
"	6th	"	"	
"	7th	"	"	
"	8th	"	"	CAMIERS
"	9th	"	"	2 N.C.O.s to Camiers for course of Instruction Hotchkiss machine Gun
"	10th	"	"	
"	11th	"	"	
"	12th	"	"	
"	13th	"	"	
"	14th	"	"	
"	15th	"	"	
LE VERTANNOY	16th	—	Proceeded to LE VERTANNOY at 10 am, arrived at about 12.30 pm. 1 N.C.O. returned from Hotchkiss machine gun Course	
"	16th	—	Divisional training. 1 Sergt & 4 men deported to H'Qrs XI Corps (HINGES) as escort for Corps Commander.	
"	19th	—	Divisional training.	attached Divnl H'Qrs with A.P.M. Kemply
"	20th	"	"	
"	21st	"	"	1 man to H'Qrs XI Corps as groom to staff officer. 1 Officer (G.E.L. BIRTH) 92? remarks

Y.G. O'Grady Capt.
O.C. 39th Divisional Cavalry & Sqdn S.I.H.

Army Form C. 2118.

WAR DIARY
or
INTELLIGENCE SUMMARY

(Erase heading not required.)

Instructions regarding War Diaries and Intelligence Summaries are contained in F. S. Regs., Part II. and the Staff Manual respectively. Title Pages will be prepared in manuscript.

Place	Date	Hour	Summary of Events and Information	Remarks and references to Appendices
LE VERTANNOY	April 22nd		Divisional training. 1 N.C.O. proceeded to LIETTRES Chateau for S.S. Elementary Signalling Course	
"	23rd		"	
"	24th		"	
"	25th		Enough of a gas attack by the Enemy was felt to make the eyes water.	
"	26th		Signal emitted by the Divisional Commander.	
"	27th		"	
"	28th		Warned by sense of a gas attack but felt no effects	
"	29th		"	
"	30th		"	

Y. O'Grady Capt
O.C. 39th Divisional Cavalry
"E" Sqdn (South Irish Horse)

2449 Wt. W4957/M90 750,000 1/16 J.B.C. & A. Forms/C.2118/12.